TRANSFORMING THE PRODIGAL SOUL

Scott Prickett

Transforming the Prodigal Soul
by Scott Prickett
Copyright ©2017
All rights reserved by M. Scott Prickett
Visit www.scottprickett.com

Printed in the United States of America.

TABLE OF CONTENTS

"Stand at the crossroads and look;

ask for the ancient paths,

ask where the good way is, and walk in it,

and you will find rest for your souls."

Jeremiah 6:16

Chapter 1

THE PRODIGAL WITHIN

There's a Bible story in Luke 15 about a young man who seeks an early inheritance from his wealthy father. The father grants the young man's request. The son, who no doubt barely glances over his shoulder as he races from his father's gates, heads to a "foreign land" where he promptly squanders his new fortune on wild living.

He goes from riches to rags in record time and soon awakens to the grim reality that he's penniless, friendless and homeless. In despair, he finds work as a farmhand responsible for feeding the pigs of a local farmer. At trough bottom, increasingly hopeless and hungry, he begins to covet the slop he's feeding the pigs.

In a moment of desperate clarity, he remembers his father and the home of abundance he left for this stark reality of lack and despair. He resolves to return home, throw himself on his father's mercy, beg forgiveness for the disrespect of his rebellion and plead for a place in the servants' quarters of his father's estate.

He heads home.

In one of the most beautiful depictions of God's love for

us, we read in Luke 15:20 "But while he was still a long way off, his father saw him and felt compassion for him, and ran and embraced him and kissed him."

We usually hear this story referred to as the Parable of the Prodigal Son, and we understand it as an analogy of our salvation experience or of God's never-ending mercy that welcomes us back when we go astray. That understanding is good and true and worth hanging onto; most of us relate to it as we often can identify times in our lives when we rebelled, suffered the consequences and ultimately returned to the safety of home.

The story of the prodigal, however, isn't just applicable to our testimonies of salvation. It is instrumental in our understanding the transformative process that is available *within* us. We can better understand the redemption of our fallen nature in exchange for the glory of God by a closer examination of the prodigal that may still reside in dark areas of our soul.

Choosing Freedom

When the prodigal son chose to return home, he was ready to accept an identity not of son but servant; to return not to his original state but a state of compromise. He was willing to consent to a life of servitude and lack instead of the life of freedom and abundance which was his birthright. The prodigal has been unleashed in the mindset of the church today. The church is full of God's sons and daughters who believe lies and ultimately choose a life of compromise and slavery rather than the Father's intended life of promise and freedom.

Our inheritance of freedom is guaranteed by Jesus' act of redemption when He died for our sins, but the realization of our freedom doesn't happen all at once. Freedom unfolds layer by layer as we work out Christ's salvation through our human condition. We are in the process of progressive redemption that requires dying to ourselves (taking up our cross daily) to allow Him to live through us.

Jesus died to free our soul from the darkness that contradicts the light of His Spirit within us. His death and resurrection make it possible to exchange our darkness for His glory, but the first requirement for exchange is possession. You can't let go of something you don't first grab hold of. If you can't admit it, you can't exchange it.

We don't realize the fullness of our capacity to live as transformed, redeemed coheirs with Christ because we say a prayer, memorize a scripture or go to a conference. As things are revealed—and they often take time and pressure to become obvious—we get to go deeper into the crevices of a soul that stores the remnant of our fallen state. When we venture courageously into the particular areas of our lives in need of personal transformation, Jesus is faithful in the little as well as the big.

With Your Heart You Believe

A disciple is born out of an encounter with Jesus, not a program or a book about Jesus. Others who've gone ahead of us can teach and build on the change He caused, but only He can facilitate the new birth that creates a disciple. The new birth of salvation is foundational to peeling back the layers of our soul and realizing freedom.

If you have any question about your salvation, don't rely on a memory of a time you got baptized or said a prayer led by someone else. Ask Jesus to reveal to you a time where you met Him, turned to Him away from where you'd been heading, and from that point forward things were different. Ask Him to show you.

If He showed you that encounter, and you have the peace of knowing you are His child, let's walk together toward the Father's home of freedom in the coming pages. If not, but there is an urge to meet Him now, ask Him if He is calling you into the salvation of new birth. The call is from Spirit to spirit; from Him to you. It is the call to new birth that means dying to you to allow Him to live in and through you. If you hear His call in your spirit, just say "Yes." With your yes to His invitation, He creates a new you where the old you used to reside.

Romans 10:9–11 says:

> *If you declare with your mouth, "Jesus is Lord," and believe in your heart that God raised him from the dead, you will be saved. For it is with your heart that you believe and are justified, and it is with your mouth that you profess your faith and are saved. As Scripture says, "Anyone who believes in him will never be put to shame."*

From the foundation of salvation, we can walk out of shame, guilt, condemnation and other lies we buy into outside of His grace. We can walk in freedom.

The Road Home

Until the prodigal parts of our soul return home to the Father's estate, those parts of us have chosen isolation and starvation over the abundance available. Desperate for sustenance and comfort, the prodigal within turns to "pig slop" served up by a foreign farmer in a place that's not our home. Only when the love of the Father floods the dark recesses of our soul do we receive clarity to see the road home and step onto it.

To realize the fullness of God's inheritance, we must

look to our own prodigal soul—the places within where we've settled for pig slop but are longing for a place at the Father's table—and then be willing to submit to the transformative power of the Father's love. It takes courage to turn toward home, but your Father will run to meet you even when you are "still a long way off." He is watching joyfully, waiting for you to return to your rightful place as His child and heir. It's time to go home.

Points to Consider

- By the grace of Jesus, we can be born again and adopted by the Father.

- Although our identity is righteous at salvation, our soul is in need of transformation.

- The prodigal aspects of our soul are feelings, thoughts and actions that don't agree with our new identity.

- Along with salvation, Jesus bought our freedom with His sacrifice.

- The transformation of our soul is the working out of our salvation.

- Where we realize an opportunity to be restored to the Father, He is faithful to meet us as we return.

Chapter 2

INVITED INTO GLORY

I am, among other things, a minister. I am called to walk with others toward freedom from bondage and toward recognition of their identity in Christ. I've spent countless hours studying, considering, praying for and ministering in freedom. I am thankful God has called me to this purpose and embrace the opportunity as an honor.

A few years ago, in the middle of this calling, I got into an argument with my wife. It was an ugly argument, and I said ugly things. What came out of me wasn't free at all. It was depraved and destructive.

Following this argument, I went into a kind of dark hole. I was embarrassed, but more than that, I was doubtful. I was full of doubt regarding the contradiction between what I believed and knew and ministered in compared to this blatant display of depravity. The fact that I had this kind of anger and venom in me caused me to question everything.

- I questioned whether or not I was a phony. If this was going to be a way I might act, is there any integrity in my ministry?

- I questioned whether or not I was disqualified. If I do these kinds of things or even if I am capable of them, am I qualified to help others?

- I questioned the very idea of freedom. If a so-called freedom minister is so full of darkness that it comes spilling out, is there even such a thing as freedom in the first place?

Those are the questions I was asking as I prayed and considered the events of the argument. The next day, I received a group text to five or six of us from a pastor friend also called to walk alongside those engaged in the quest for freedom. He explained in his text that he needed prayer as he'd lost his temper in his home the night before. The aftermath of his anger was evident in damaged relationships and broken trust.

Almost instinctively, I typed a text in response. My response to him was, "You win. By raising your hand, inviting us in and sending this text, you win." That was it. That was the answer to my questions.

Freedom isn't the absence of sin but the willingness to expose darkness to light. Freedom isn't living a perfect life, but living life's imperfections with others to disarm the accusations of guilt and shame arising from our faults. Freedom is simply the ability to raise your hand. Raising your hand is the first step on the return journey to an inheritance that abounds beyond our limitations.

Our Faults Invite Freedom

In Romans 7:15, the Apostle Paul wrote, "I do not understand what I do. For what I want to do I do not do, but what I hate I do." The Holy Spirit chose a guy who was jacked up to write a significant portion of the Bible. Paul wasn't perfect even after his radical, blinding-light conversion. He was a murdering, Christ-hater prior to the encounter, and he was still doing things that he hated after salvation. For those of us that realize our own imperfection, that should be encouraging.

The exact same guy also wrote "Now the Lord is the Spirit, and where the Spirit of the Lord is, there is freedom" in 2 Corinthians 3:17. From reading his letters to the church, we know Paul's life was very similar to most of ours. Like Paul, our lives are fraught with contradiction and inner conflict. He was a pioneer in freedom questing and left us a Bible overflowing with directions, instructions and encouragement for the journey.

We learn from Paul, from fellow travelers and from our own experience that faults don't invalidate freedom; they invite it. What we do doesn't disqualify us; it invites the One that qualifies us. The grace of Jesus Christ transforms behaviors; it doesn't disqualify us based on them. We're invited into the transformation that works out Him through us so those things I described about myself, that my friend texted about himself and that the Apostle Paul writes about himself are exchanged for God's glory.

It Will Cost You Everything

Paul wrote in Philippians 2:12, "Therefore, my dear friends, as you have always obeyed—not only in my presence but now much more in my absence—continue to work out your salvation with fear and trembling."

If you've been born again by accepting Jesus as Savior and allowing His transformation in your life, there is a process of working out that salvation. When we receive Him, He resides at our core, in our spirit. The issues we all struggle with, however, are in our soul. Working out our salvation is dying to our soulish nature, so His Spirit's glory, which resides within us, is seen more clearly.

His glory will not be denied; the only question is whether you will accept His invitation to be part of the unfolding glories. Regretfully, most of the American church is neither seeking nor accepting invitations. Most often we're far too comfortable lounging in our salvation, waiting for heaven, just trying to "be good" in the meantime. We don't readily pursue a personal realization of heaven coming to earth from our places of relative comfort.

Why do we turn down an invitation into glory from the same God who saved us? Because it's hard to step into invitations that reveal new glory. Between the former glory and the new glory, there's a distinct level of discomfort, if not outright suffering. That struggle between glories shapes our character to increase our capacity to steward the new glory.

You're invited, and it will cost you everything, a little bit at a time. The faults of your soul giving way to the glory of His Spirit within you cost the crucifixion of everything within that isn't Him. It can be painful but glorious as more of Him comes out through less of you.

Dark is Dark; People are People

My path to vocational ministry is non-traditional. Leading up to this transition in my occupation, I worked previously as an Army officer, business manager and owner as well as an attorney at law. When I first practiced law, my primary focus was in the sphere of criminal defense. The bulk of that criminal defense practice was representing court-appointed clients. These were folks charged with a crime who couldn't afford an attorney.

In those days when I talked about work or now when I tell

stories about that time, some people have a noticeable reaction. They make a face, however subtle, that indicates they can't pay attention to the details because they are distracted by the arrangement. "How could you represent those people? They aren't Christians, and you are, so how could you represent them?" Many times, it's just the look, but sometimes it's explicitly asked. Church polite, of course, but asked just the same.

By contrast, one day walking out of the courthouse I called my wife and told her, "I can't believe more Christians don't choose the practice of law as their place of calling." After all, I reasoned, where else are you in a position where broken, desperate people come to you asking for your counsel and assistance? Where else is light so necessary than in the darkest places of society?

Working closely with those whose lives were in peril of being consumed by darkness gave me a greater appreciation for light. We all need some realization of darkness to remind us of the Light within. We also need some realization of darkness to remind us of the darkness within. The degree of separation between "them" and "us" is less than you might imagine. A twist here and a turn there in life's circumstances can lead people into situations both unplanned for and undesired.

The overlap in working with "church folks" and court-appointed folks is more similar than you might think, as well. Sure, most of the church folks in the relatively privileged suburbs present themselves better than the accused of the court-appointed criminal justice system. The underlying human condition, however, is just as dark. People are people.

Here, however, is the biggest difference: Those accused and convicted of crimes realize the urgency and near hopelessness of their condition. They know they need help. They know they're messed up and more often than not are desperate for any glimmer of hope. The socially acceptable, comfortable Christians often think they have things figured out. They rationalize that Jesus loves them regardless, and nobody (they hope) knows about their "indiscretions." And after all, their flaws aren't as "bad" as the indigent criminal; likely not even perceived to be as bad as the rumors they've heard—and helped spread—about the guy across the pew.

Dark is dark and pretending it's light by shades of comparison cheapens the grace of Jesus Christ. He didn't die for us to be judgmental by comparison or dismissive of the heart in need of redemption. He wants to transform us from glory to glory, but we can't go to the next glory believing the glory we've already experienced somehow jumped us ahead to a place of superiority.

The invitation into glory isn't an offer of country club

membership, and responding requires far more than a sinner's prayer RSVP. As you accept the invitation, you get the privilege of walking the road to freedom side by side with an assortment of others, and though the path isn't always smooth, your Father always makes a way of passage. Don't get discouraged. He's already headed down the road to meet you.

Points to Consider

- There is more to the Christian life and calling than saying a prayer and going to church.

- There is an opportunity for walking out a faith that is life-altering in every way.

- The cost for such a faith is everything, but the return on that investment is infinite.

- There is no measure to the glory into which Jesus invites us if we're willing to release the taste of glory we've already experienced.

- Our first step in appropriating this new glory is realizing we are limited and flawed.

- Next, we must utterly believe God is good and He is for us.

Chapter 3
ESTABLISHING THE CORE

There was a time I was facilitating a small group at a "halfway house," a safe place for men transitioning from trouble related to addiction go to get their feet under them to walk a new path. Many times residents of such houses have spent time in prison, some more recently than others. Naturally, that experience and the events that led them to that point shape their perspective, so one major challenge for many is getting beyond those experiences and events as indicators of their identity.

I saw this play out during a meeting as one of the older men, who had spent significant time in prison, consistently referred to himself and the group generally as "convicts." After a while, one of the younger guys in the group chimed in. This young man, who had also spent time in prison, was visibly agitated at the relentless reference to him by association as a "convict." He said to the older man, "I'm not a convict, and I don't want to be called a convict anymore so stop saying that." Despite the facts (he had been convicted), he was trumpeting the truth (what he had done wasn't who he is).

While it resulted in a slightly tense moment, the confrontation was critical for the survival of the younger man's hope. He was declaring that his destiny is greater than his experience; that his identity is not what others call him, but rather what he is called by the One who declared his identity when He created him.

It doesn't take a halfway house, prison or other circumstances so drastic for us to fall into the trap of labels and identities that are counterfeits and lies compared to the truth of who we are created to be. From our spirit, we're intended to know our identity, but one consequence of the fall of Adam is we are born with persistent questions regarding who we are.

Our Original Design

Genesis 2:7 recounts the creation of man and describes it in detail as, "Then the Lord God formed a man from the dust of the ground and breathed into his nostrils the breath of life and the man became a living being." From this passage, we see the formation of man into three parts.

- Man was formed in the flesh by the dust of the ground. The skin package, our flesh that holds the person, is a creation of dirt.

- God then breathed into the dirt suit and gave man His Spirit; man became a spirit after God's image.

- The net result is man became a living being, or literally translated a living "soul." With the breath of God, Adam became a living soul.

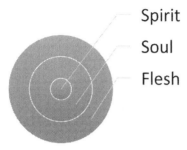

Spirit

Soul

Flesh

God breathed His Spirit into us at our core. It's the spirit part of us that is the very image of our Father, our true self. The word transliterated for "soul" in Genesis 2 is *nephesh,* and is defined as containing three parts; the will, the mind and the emotions[1], so a more detailed diagram of our design looks like this:

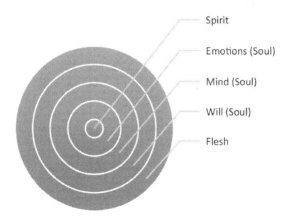

Spirit

Emotions (Soul)

Mind (Soul)

Will (Soul)

Flesh

Where the Spirit of God dwelt in our original design and is still intended to live within us at our core, we are born orphans with no inkling of our true lineage or purpose. This void in our core is critical to the actions and reactions of our soul as we live. A lifetime of mistaken identity can persist in our perception and consciousness even after we accept the salvation offered by Christ that restores the Father's Spirit at our center.

Before salvation our attempts to fill this emptiness may drive us to extremes of addiction or other unhealthy behaviors. After salvation these behaviors can continue to be roadblocks on our soul's journey back to the Father. Understanding how the three parts of our being (Diagram 1) and the three parts of our soul (Diagram 2) interact is key to overcoming these obstacles.

From Submitting Son to Self-Reliant Soul

Leading up to the fall of man, God warned Adam if he ate from the tree of knowledge of good and evil he would die. Subsequently, the serpent slithered in and directly challenged God's word in Genesis 3:4, telling Eve "You will not certainly die." After the disobedient eating of the forbidden fruit, Adam and Eve continued to walk around, living and breathing. Somebody lied. God said they would die and the serpent said they wouldn't, and they undoubtedly continued to exist even after their disobedience. Did God lie? Of course not.

After the fall, the source of life within Adam was no longer the Spirit of God because it was now separated from Adam's soul by his choice to rebel. Adam went from a selfless, submitting son, dependent on the Spirit's guidance at his core, to a selfish, insecure, little "g" god in his own right, idolatrous as it was.

When Adam rebelled, he rejected the indwelling love of the Father and became a soulish creature. He went from knowing he was God's son because God the Father reminded him from the inside out to being self-reliant. That's the challenging inheritance we all received from Adam: self-reliance.

In the exchange of Genesis 3:8–11, we see with painful clarity the changed reality from which Adam relates to God. No longer based on the gloriously confident trust found in the truth of God's breath within him, Adam's newly acquired knowledge has changed his reality from one of sonship to one of self-centered creature.

> *Then the man and his wife heard the sound of the Lord God as he was walking in the garden in the cool of the day, and they hid from the Lord God among the trees of the garden.*
>
> *But the Lord God called to the man, "Where are you?"*

He answered, "I heard you in the garden, and I was afraid because I was naked; so I hid."

And he said, "Who told you that you were naked? Have you eaten from the tree that I commanded you not to eat from?"

With the eating of the fruit, Adam's soul instantly became focused on the revelation of his limitations, and it left him exposed. Shame and fear overcame him, and he did what we all do, he hid. What was once Father and son walking together in the cool of the day became man running from God in a futile attempt to hide his sin.

Obviously, God always knew where Adam was. He gave Adam a chance to recognize his need for repentance by allowing him to see and acknowledge his condition. He prompted it with the question of "Where are you?" From a distant pig slop, the prodigal in our soul still hears the Father's call of "Where are you?" Just as Adam, we are afforded the opportunity to consider our condition and acknowledge our need to turn home, if we will.

Driving the Behavior

Adam admitted his fear and God's response was to take him to the lie that drove his behavior. The behavior was Adam hiding from God in shame, but there was more to the story. There always is. When God asked him who told him he was naked, it wasn't because God didn't know. God wanted Adam to know because understanding the origin of false beliefs about God or about ourselves is crucial to discovering our true identity as God's children and ultimately finding our way home to freedom.

Alcoholics don't drink too much because they're thirsty; there's more to the story that drives the behavior. Addiction and other excess is driven by a void in the soul. That void originates in lack of identity and grows because of lack of intimacy. Both these needs are God-breathed, but are legitimately filled only by connection to the Father who informs us who we are and provides supreme intimacy at our core when His Spirit resides there. False beliefs about God or about ourselves prevent us from returning home to connect with Him in that part of our soul.

To stem the destructive results of our excess we often resort to more and more restrictive sets of rules. These updated versions of the Old Covenant of the Law produce the same deadly results. There is no freedom in the discipline of good behavior by following rules; freedom comes from the transformation of desire.

We have to look deeper, beyond the behavior to find the lie we bought into if we want to disarm the power of the destructive patterns in our lives. Lies hide in the dark, frightening crevices of our soul we'd rather pretend don't exist even as the call to freedom insists we "go there."

Going Home From Within

Because of Adam's rebellion, we are born to a life of death, separated from God and wallowing in a pigsty of self-reliant inadequacy. Born again, we are a new spirit, one again with our Father; our identity is restored as children of God. Our soul and flesh, however, are not reborn. We are still dealing with a runaway, prodigal soul that struggles to do its own thing in contrast to the direction of God's Spirit within us.

We are born into rebellion but with a merciful invitation to return home to the Father who loves us and wants to be the Source of life from within. In Isaiah God promises never to forget we are His children, no matter how far from home we roam. "Can a mother forget the baby at her breast and have no compassion on the child she has borne? Though she may forget, I will not forget you! See, I have engraved you on the palms of my hands" (Isaiah 49:15–16). Even in our prodigal state, our Father stands on the road and calls "Where are you?" then lovingly waits for us to hear, turn and head home.

God's Spirit living in us is Holy and Righteous, making us also holy and righteous, and is our intended dwelling place. It is home. We are to dwell with the Father within us, finding His peace at our center, even in the turmoil of a world full of trouble and a flesh bent toward temptation. Home with the Father is where we started, in Adam, and where we can finish, through Jesus.

Jesus makes available the connection to the Father that allows us to walk with Him in the cool of the day once again. The beautiful mystery of our return to the Garden of Eden is that the Garden isn't restored around us; it's restored within us. We don't immediately leave the world, but heaven immediately comes and dwells within us, and we become spiritual beings as always intended.

The restoration of the Father's estate is the return to the Father's Spirit within us, and we go home from within. He establishes His place within us through the sacrifice and invitation of Jesus who paid the price for Adam's rebellion. The Father's estate becomes our refuge, and we find sanctuary in the peace of knowing His love at our core. In the example of the prodigal, consider it like this:

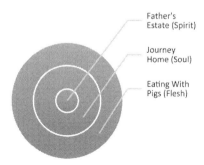

Father's
Estate (Spirit)

Journey
Home (Soul)

Eating With
Pigs (Flesh)

Failure to acknowledge and trust in the Father's love in areas of our lives produces the voids that harbor prodigals in our soul. Searching out and exposing these runaways is difficult because our feelings and thoughts will fool us. The prodigal son in Luke believed wholeheartedly he was right and justified in receiving his inheritance. He most likely was passionate about that belief. It wasn't until hunger and wretchedness forced him to survey the consequences of his choices that he was able to accurately assess that returning to the father was both good and right.

Until awareness of his father's love and goodness was highlighted by the manifestation of his will and the accompanying ramifications, he couldn't go home. First, he had to look around and honestly assess his circumstances, as his will produced undeniable proof through his fleshly choices. The prodigals in our soul are revealed in much the same way, if we have the fortitude to honestly examine the evidence.

Points to Consider

- When we are born again, we are righteous and holy in our spirit as His Spirit comes to dwell within us.

- Our flesh and soul, however, are still on their prodigal journey as our natural state of rebellion requires redemption.

- Voids in our soul lead to excess as we attempt to fill

legitimate needs through illegitimate means. These excesses manifest in various behaviors contradictory to the Truth of who we are and Who God is.

- We don't know the condition of our soul until we survey our behaviors and choices and their consequences.

- Our souls are invited to align with His Spirit within us and transformation is available for as long as we are increasingly willing to return.

Chapter 4

EVIDENCE OF THE FLESH

I once had a court-appointed client facing charges that could result in up to one year in jail. He was almost an hour late to court and the judge kept waiting as his name was called numerous times. Finally came the fifth and final call and he was there. I asked the judge for a minute to confer with him outside the courtroom, and she agreed. When we got into the hallway, it went something like this:

> "You are off to a bad start. This is the toughest judge in this city, and she knows you're late because your name has been called numerous times. It's important to be on time and show you're taking this seriously. The judge likely won't be happy that you don't seem to be responsible enough or interested enough to get here on time," I explained.

> "I want a new lawyer," he instantly responded.

> "Okay, let's go in there and ask for you to get a new lawyer (the judge had to approve that request)," I said as I grabbed the door handle back toward the courtroom. Pausing before opening the door, I asked, "Why do you want a new lawyer?"

"Because you aren't helping me."

"Yes, I am; you just aren't happy that I'm holding you accountable. I was never disrespectful to you, and I looked you in the eye and was direct with you. You're just not used to being dealt with directly, and now you don't like it, so you want a different lawyer. Let's go ask the judge."

Almost as instantly as he'd thought to dismiss me, he reached out and grabbed my arm and said, "Wait a minute. I want you to be my lawyer."

Just like that, this 50-something-year-old man responded to the candor of the investment I was attempting to make in him. It appeared almost an involuntary reflex for him to grab my arm and decide he would stick with me. It was almost an afterthought that he would trust my advocacy and believe I was for him. In that moment, he decided to receive the direct and challenging critique I offered him.

Prior to my frank assessment of him, that man believed he was "okay." Right up to the point of my looking him in the eye and telling him the truth about himself, he was deceived and unaware of the need to consider his culpability in his current circumstances. Only when confronted by the truth about himself was he able to stop blaming me or somebody else for the actions that brought him to this point, facing the prospect of dismal consequences meted out by an unhappy judge.

Recognizing the Prodigals

The journey home for the prodigal soul takes place on the inside but is verified on the outside. Even as we know that we know we are children of God, from His Spirit to ours, our soul struggles. Mostly it struggles with accepting the promise of His provision, protection and promotion where there is capacity for self-reliance. Our soul relentlessly wrestles with contentment in the rest of God when action produces more immediate satisfaction. Those areas where our soul prevails in our decision-making over His Spirit's invitation to trust and wait are areas in which we have not returned home. They are prodigals.

There's often evidence in my behavior that contradicts Christ's perfection within me. That's the soulish and fleshly part of me that's still being made holy. Working out our salvation is the process of transformation that occurs within our soul toward our increasing holiness. We don't have to will ourselves holy. We get to be holy because Jesus says we are, and what's in our soul that disagrees can be submitted to His truth within us. So how do we recognize the prodigals in our soul so we can turn them toward home?

If we look only at our soul, we'll deceive ourselves. It doesn't take a great prophet to know our mind, will and emotions are subject to volatility and error, although one of the greatest confirmed it for us: "The heart is deceitful above all things and beyond cure. Who can understand it?" (Jeremiah 17:9). The word transliterated for "heart" in Jeremiah is the Hebrew *leb,* and means "inner man, mind, will, heart."[2] It's the soul. Other translations of Jeremiah 17:9 imply the soul is not only deceitful but also sick. Starting from a sick, deceitful soul, we'd be on shaky ground in the quest to work out our salvation and be transformed to be more like Christ.

We have a flesh with a bent toward self-indulgence, and the experience of a life lived in a fallen world fuels that bent. As we live, hurts and disappointments foster lies that validate the already perverted desires of the flesh. When that happens, we not only have the pull of the flesh but the fuel of the lies that drive the flesh toward destructive choices. Thus, the prodigal is unleashed.

The Believer's Duty of Candor

Our flesh pulls us to temporal satisfaction of eternal needs, and the Father awaits our return. His house is better than the places our flesh takes us, but something still drives us to choose poorly. That "something" is a stronghold of false belief fueling our poor choices. To determine what those strongholds are, we can't start at the soul because it will lie to us. We first have to examine our behaviors to determine whether or not they are based on truth or lies. We have to consider our sin.

This book is based on the premise you've been born again through the sacrifice of Jesus Christ. It's for believers. Believers must examine and deal with their sin to realize the promise of the Father's dwelling within us. Salvation isn't the end of the journey; it's the beginning. The fulfillment of freedom isn't automatic; it's a process.

To look at our sin, we have to know what sin is and what sin isn't. Scripture gives us the framework of God's intentions for us. Viewing our choices through this framework reveals those areas where the two fail to align. Bible study isn't for the sake of knowledge to impress other Christians. Bible study is critical to our freedom because only when we know where we're out of alignment with God's design can we make the corrections necessary to get back on target.

In the practice of law, there is a duty of "candor to the tribunal." In other words, there is an ethical obligation to be entirely truthful to the court. Lawyers can't present subjective perceptions, opinions or ideas as law or fact. There is no room for deception or misrepresentation of any kind. If your integrity is in question, your license to practice law is in jeopardy.

Christ followers have that same duty of candor if they desire to walk in the fullness of freedom and purpose into which Jesus invites them. We can't twist, justify or compare the evidence of our choices to avoid the forthrightness required for an evaluation of our soul.

> *"If we say we have no sin, we deceive ourselves, and the truth is not in us. If we confess our sins, he is faithful and just to forgive us our sins and to cleanse us from all unrighteousness. If we say we have not sinned, we make him a liar, and his word is not in us" (1 John 1:8–10).*

Our Choices Reflect Our Will

Just before the fall of Cain in Genesis 4, Cain had an opportunity to stop the progression of his sin. Cain was warned of pending destruction as God noticed Cain had a bad attitude resulting from his discontentment with his lack of blessing compared to Abel's good fortune. If Cain had been willing to honestly examine himself at the presentation of sin, which actually started with his unwillingness to give his first and best to God, maybe things would have ended differently.

In Genesis 4:6–7, God tells Cain:

> *Then the Lord said to Cain, "Why are you angry? Why is your face downcast? If you do what is right, will you not be accepted? But if you do not do what is right, sin is crouching at your door; it desires to*

have you, but you must rule over it."

Cain, however, was unwilling to rule over the impulses of his soul. He allowed his discontentment to turn to anger and result in murder.

Honesty about our present is necessary to realize the promise of our future. Jesus came to redeem all things, but again, we can't exchange what we won't own. Our choices reflect our will, despite our beliefs about our intentions. Sick, deceitful hearts can't be trusted, but the evidence of our will is foolproof in the choices we make that manifest in the hard evidence of our flesh. If we own them, we can be free of what caused them.

We choose as we believe. We can say we believe in the love of the Father, the grace of Jesus and the fellowship of Holy Spirit, but if we actually believe, our choices will verify our declaration. Belief isn't about our knowledge; it's about our will.

To achieve the freedom available where the Spirit of God dwells within us, we have to start from a place we know without question. Since our soul will lie to us according to Jeremiah 17:9, we need the hard, cold facts of our flesh. The choices we make reveal without a doubt where, when and why our soul is siding with the flesh over His spirit within us.

It may be hard to look at, and the temptation will be to justify or discount the testimony of the flesh, but if I were your lawyer, I'd advise you to take the evidence seriously. However painful it may be, your candid examination of the evidence is vital for your successful journey home to complete freedom.

Points to Consider

- The working out of our salvation is the process of transformation that begins with looking at the desires of our flesh which contradict God's Spirit within us.

- Our way home starts by simply turning away from those things we know are not based in truth and allowing the process of God's transforming love to begin.

- The journey to freedom begins with a candid assessment of our sins. Our imperfections are clues to how to move forward.

- Despite what we believe about our "good intentions," we must accept the hard evidence of our flesh as indicators of prodigals in our soul. Only then can we submit them to the grace of Jesus and turn them back to the Father.

- Our belief in God is only as valid as our willingness to admit our faith in His ability to transform those things about us that are not of Him.

Chapter 5

CHOICES REFLECT THE WILL

I came out of the gym one morning, and there was a guy in the parking lot who, judging by his clothes, had either just finished working out or was about to go in to work out. He was standing in the parking lot smoking a cigarette which struck me as kind of funny. The contradiction is obvious as related to the healthy versus the unhealthy activity since one is presumably a positive behavioral choice while the other is an addictive negative behavior.

Contradictions in conduct such as I observed that day outside the gym sometimes are referred to as duplicity, the existence of more than one expression of our character. We all battle duplicity at one level or another and difficult life circumstances often make the battle much more challenging. For Christians, this particular battle also leads to secondary skirmishes with guilt or confusion or doubt, very much as I experienced after the dark-hole argument with my wife I alluded to at the beginning of this book.

At the moment of salvation, the supernatural power of Christ's Spirit transforms us into a new person in our spirit. From that moment, we're a new creature at our very core. The conversion of our soul, as we've seen, isn't so instantaneous. In working out our salvation, we acknowledge our identity has been changed at its core, but our soul is still battling this new nature for control. Knowledge is a powerful weapon in any battle. Understanding how each part of our soul operates as well as how they work in conjunction helps us rein in the prodigal aspects of our soul so we can submit them to the transformative power of Holy Spirit.

Working Through This Holy Friction

The truth of the Father dwelling within us by His Spirit is a challenging reality based on the facts as we see them and the duplicity we are far too aware of in our flesh and soul. In the mirror, we see a guy in athletic attire, smoking cigarettes in the gym parking lot, even as the Spirit assures us that's not who we are. The battle is to overcome the natural, perceptible senses so we can realize the supernatural, invisible promises.

Look at Hebrews 10:14. "For by one sacrifice, he has made perfect forever those who are being made holy." You don't have to be an English professor to recognize something about that sentence just doesn't "read right." "Has made perfect" is past tense and "being made holy" is present and ongoing.

So, how does something that has already happened keep

on happening? Because the thing that *has happened* in our spirits *is happening* in our souls. The seeming discord of Hebrews 10:14 resolves completely when we consider that our spirit is clothed in righteousness through Jesus even as parts of our soul are dressed in gym clothes smelling of cigarette smoke.

The battleground for freedom is within our soul and how well that battle is going is reflected in our will, the outermost ring of the soul's anatomy. To get a clear picture of the condition of our soul, we must look at the choices reflected by our will.

It Is What It Is

There was a time I had a client appointed to me after he'd pled guilty to a pretty serious charge. My job was to represent him through the sentencing phase. Considering his background, the presentencing assessment completed and provided to the judge, and the statute, there was a prescribed range for his sentence. The judge could vary from the guidelines, but this judge in this jurisdiction wasn't going to. The final sentence was going to land right in the middle.

My client didn't have a criminal background and wasn't accustomed to being in trouble. I surmised he either wasn't in the habit of breaking the law or hadn't gotten caught until now because, despite his persona of respectability, his felonious actions had him facing some grave consequences. He instructed me to ask the judge to drop below the sentencing guidelines based on the fact that he was a "good guy," had a good job, good family; all the trappings of "respectable" citizen.

All those variables had been factored into the presentencing report and the guidelines to the degree they could be quantified. The consequences for the offense of which my client was convicted were objective and left no leeway for the subjectivity of his self-asserted intentions. I knew there wasn't going to be a downward departure from the guidelines, but I made the motion, just the same.

As predicted, the judge denied it, but not out of spite. The judge just wasn't in the habit of circumventing the instruction of the law to guess at the motives of those whose criminal acts landed them before her bench. The facts clearly showed the court the defendant's motives. It didn't take guesswork to determine what he wanted to do based on what he did.

Belief Equals Trust

The same is true for you and me. As much as we want to be judged based on "pure motives," the hard truth is our motives are only as wholesome as the choices we make. We can pretend the muck that comes out of us doesn't reflect us, but that's an illusion. Most of us possess at least some virtue inside that indeed seems to argue against the contrary choices that bring consequences, but our choices speak more definitively than our intentions. What we do reflects our beliefs, even if we are in church every week and better than we used to be or better, by comparison, than the guy next door.

Our choices reflect our will, the part of our soul most closely associated with our flesh. We know what we want by observing what we choose. If we say we believe, intend or desire one thing but then choose another, the thing we choose is the most accurate reflection of what we truly believe or really want at that moment. It's objective, not subjective.

We form beliefs in the laws of nature by assessing verifiable facts, such as observing an object fall and developing a belief in the veracity of the law of gravity. We base our spiritual beliefs on spiritual truths, not necessarily as easily recognizable to the senses but just as evident in practice. Belief in something is the practice of trust that shows up in our choices. It's this simple: If you believe something will fall because of the immutable law of gravity, you'll hold onto it; if you trust God will hold onto you because of His incontrovertible word and character, you'll rest in Him.

Our faith—or lack thereof—is manifest in evidence of

our actions and behaviors, not simply ideas or knowledge about Scripture. Hebrews 11:1 tells us our faith will have substance to it.[3] It will be tangible. We won't just say we believe; we'll act in belief. The evidence of our faith will be available for others to make a case for—or against—our God through the choices of our will.

Honestly Assessing Our Faith

Belief in God is not the mastery of information about God, but trusting Him to be God for us. We not only believe He is sovereign over the universe, but we submit to His sovereignty in our choices. Those things that show up in our behaviors that don't reflect Him are areas where we don't believe Him. We have chosen our own way out of rebellion, immaturity or both.

Stepping into freedom begins with an honest assessment of the evidence of our beliefs as demonstrated by the choices we make. What do your choices say you believe about God? About yourself? If your choices are missing the mark (sin) from the intention and design of your true identity, they are evidence of a stronghold. We'll delve more deeply into strongholds later, but a stronghold is an area of your soul that's been taken captive by a lie so must be liberated by God's truth.

As we honestly assess our actions and repent, we accept Jesus' invitation and begin to turn toward home, away from choices driven by beliefs contrary to His truth. This step requires submitting our will long enough to grant Him permission to commune with the rest of our soul (mind and emotions) so they can be transformed by His presence. It's our part of drawing near to Him that we read about in James 4:8, "Come near to God, and He will come near to you. Wash your hands, you sinners, and purify your hearts, you double-minded."

We're all double-minded. None of us have life figured out so perfectly that there's never a remnant of the prodigal not crowding its way into our choices. That double-minded tug-of-war can wreak havoc on our peace and hijack our destiny if we allow it. We're being called continually deeper, into a more and more profound return to the Father's estate, where He and He alone resides. Our double-minded doubt, fear and other hesitations cannot live there, in the presence of His love.

Our first step on the way home doesn't have to be particularly well thought out. All we have to do is start that direction, submitting our will to Him, trusting He'll meet us as we turn. James 4:8 promises He will.

Points to Consider

- We are all double-minded to some degree or another and this duplicity in our soul is reflected in our will.

- We believe as we choose, despite any inner conflict we experience over those choices.

- The soul is the battleground of our design where we choose to live according to God's Spirit and truth or our fear and selfishness.

- God's love allows us to reject His invitations and experience the consequences of our choices.

- By experiencing those consequences, we consider the invitation of God's goodness and reconsider submitting our will to His Spirit.

- Submitting our will allows His Spirit to transform the deeper layers of our soul.

Chapter 6

LOVE CHANGES OUR MIND

Our mind is Soul Central. Every behavior that manifests through our will to our flesh has at its core a thought, a belief. That belief may correspond to an emotional experience, but every action of our will is preceded by a thought. Our mind exists as the connector between our emotions, the inner, most elusive aspect of our soul, and our will, the outer, most evident layer.

The journey to freedom is one of transformation. The prodigal parts of our soul are changed more and more as they draw closer to the Father. According to Romans 12:2, our mind is where this transformation occurs: "Do not conform to the pattern of this world, but be transformed by the renewing of your mind. Then you will be able to test and approve what God's will is—his good, pleasing and perfect will."

The renewing of our mind allows us to see ourselves as God sees us and the transformation begins. A renewed mind allows us to understand His perfect will and thereby choose behaviors that reflect His will over ours.

Because we are transformed by the renewal of our mind, it is the critical juncture in the redemption of our soul. It is in our mind that the emotion of fear (which we will examine in greater detail in the next chapter) is either fostered and given destructive rule in our choices through our will or transformed into faith by submitting it to the healing presence of the Father's love.

The Cross-Road of Doubt

The first intersection we overcome in our mind is doubt. Doubt is the cross-road believers encounter time after time as we travel toward home. It's that point on the road where we must choose to trust our Father, despite what we see in front of us that might contradict His guidance, or to rely on our soul's decision-making over His Spirit's call and direction.

All believers face doubt somewhere along their journey. In Matthew 28, the very guys Jesus commissioned to carry the Kingdom to the world were worshiping him "but some doubted" (v. 17). Jesus commissioned them anyway. One of those commissioned was Peter, the only person besides Jesus to ever walk on water.

> *Then Peter got down out of the boat, walked on the water and came toward Jesus. But when he saw the wind, he was afraid and, beginning to sink, cried out, "Lord, save me!" Immediately Jesus reached out his hand and caught him. "You of little faith," he said, "why did you doubt?" (Matthew 14:29–31).*

The word for "doubt" in Matthew 28:17 and Matthew 14:31 is the transliteration of the Greek "*distazo.*" These are the only two times in the New Testament that word is used. Think about the irony. The two scenes for this particular sort of doubting were the tangible presence of the risen Christ, whom many of the doubters saw die and be buried, and at experiencing a man walking on water. In the middle of two of the most supernatural manifestations imaginable, there was doubt among those witnessing these miracles. Apparently, we're in good company when challenged by doubt.

In each case, the doubt that tested these men was a question of focus more than evidence. They took their eyes off the realization of the supernatural and chose to concentrate on the natural. The natural raised questions that opposed the reality of the glory of God in their midst.

Doubt Doesn't Disqualify

Peter's water-top trip was cut short by doubt, but not his lifelong journey of discipleship. His moment of doubt had no bearing on his invitation into relationship with Jesus, just as it had no bearing on the call of the other ten disciples sent to spread the Gospel of Christ to the world. Doubt does not equal disqualification. It isn't the cause; it's the effect. It's the result of a stair-stepped progression whose foundation is fear, something like this:

- Doubt is a product of focus
  - Focus is a product of choice
    - Choice is driven by desire
      - Desire can be hijacked by fear
        - Fear is the absence of love

Doubt isn't a rejection of God; in fact, the tension and argument within us are an affirmation of our belief in God. If we didn't believe He was there, we wouldn't entertain the conversation. Doubt isn't a manifestation of sin until and unless we choose unbelief.

Doubt is a question of whether the Father is going to come through for us. It's a question of whether we believe He loves us enough to take care of us. It's a question of trust. The prodigal soul has to trust that the Father's love is extended in grace through Jesus, despite the whispers of disqualification based on specific sins committed. Anything else is unbelief.

It Starts with Asking "Why?"

The transformation of our soul depends on the renewal of our mind. We ask "Why?" regarding our choices, and then assess what our beliefs apparently were in the moments we chose as we did. When I say "we ask why," we ask ourselves, but must rely on the revelation of Holy Spirit.

It goes something like this, "Holy Spirit, why do I do the thing I hate (filling in the blank of that 'thing' with whatever persistent temptation(s) trips you up)?" Then listen and wait. Embrace solitude and silence to allow for the whispers of God to reveal the absence of God in your beliefs.

Concealed within those God-deficient beliefs that drive sin, there is a lie. Until uncovered, you don't know it's a lie because it's normal to you. You've acclimated to it. That's why we don't start within our soul, but first look at the indisputable evidence of our flesh that demonstrates our will in our behaviors. Once uncovered by subjecting it in our mind to the truth of God's Word, we can exchange lies and false beliefs for the truth. That's the essence of redemption.

The truth of Scripture is available to replace the lies which take root in life's hurts, disappointments, accusations and failures. The genuine transformation of our mind is moving from understanding a theory about who God is to actually embracing our identity in Him. We exchange our false ideas of identity for His truth of our lineage and design. We move from concepts and lessons *about* God to identity *in* Him as Father. We are His children, and we can increasingly know our place in His house.

Identity Restored by Truthful Thinking

Once I was representing a young man who had a string of criminal problems. I met his mother outside the courtroom as she waited for him to be brought out in the orange jumpsuit and stand this most recent trial. She had lost hope for him. She told me "I've come to the conclusion he's just a criminal."

That statement was a lie she had come to believe about a son she undoubtedly loved. She believed the lie because one disappointment after another suggested the identity of "criminal" could be the only appropriate label. If the young man's mother thought that and spoke it to and about her son, how long before he bought the lie (if he hadn't already)?

That young man wasn't created to be a criminal. No one is created to be a criminal. As I told that defeated mother, something went wrong to get this boy off track; getting off track resulted in bad decisions that brought about consequences which undoubtedly reinforced things that were off track in the first place.

So many criminal defendants, particularly when there are minor violations, want to avoid a conviction because they want to "keep it off my record." The "record" becomes an indicator of their identity. The things people have done become defining markers that support conclusions skimmed from the surface of the individual. The depth of who they are gets lost in the suggestion of the record of offenses juxtaposed against their intended destiny.

Redemption takes that record and makes it irrelevant. Grace is the supernatural white-out that covers every conviction, mistake or bad choice. Identity is restored as the truth of what God says replaces what others say about us or we say about ourselves. The mind is renewed when it is afforded the grace to agree with God's design for us. His design is for us to walk in purpose toward the accomplishment of great and glorious things. Anything short of that is a lie in need of redemption.

When Love and Repentance Collide

As we start home to the promise of the Father, we first submit our will by recognizing and turning from the sin we chose previously. We turn to Him to examine why we were doing the things we hate in the first place, and we find the lies we believed. The Father starts toward us as soon as we start back, meeting us in our repentance and restoring us to truth.

He meets us at the intersection of our mind, even in our doubt, and provides the truth of His Word and the revelation of His Spirit to replace the lies. The collision of His unconditional love with our authentic repentance triggers the transformation of our thinking. This transformation continues as we embrace the truth about who we are and continue home, past wounds and emotions that have clouded our view.

The detailed description of the prodigal's reunion with his father as told in Luke 15:20 provides us an understanding of how our minds are transformed when we head home: "So he got up and went to his father. But while he was still a long way off, his father saw him and was filled with compassion for him; he ran to his son, threw his arms around him and kissed him."

The prodigal was far away, but the father recognized him even before he came into full view. The moment he recognized him, he ran. Colliding with his son in the middle of the road, the father kissed him, the breath of his mouth and nostrils no doubt covering the prodigal's face and neck as his father embraced him.

The runaway's trip didn't end with him standing dejectedly at his father's doorstep, knocking fearfully for admittance as a slave. It ended in the middle of the road, in an embrace so full of acceptance and affection that it immediately transformed his thoughts. All his imaginings of a strained, painful encounter with an angry patriarch followed by a lifetime of servitude dissolved as he experienced the breath of his loving father on his skin as they embraced.

Agreeing With Father

The prodigal's journey home was neither as long nor as frightening as he'd imagined. Neither is ours. As soon as we change our mind about behaviors we've embraced and turn from them to accept the invitation into the Kingdom in that area of our lives, the Father runs to us from the place He dwells within us, our spirits. His love collides with our repentance in the midst of the journey, He embraces us, and His Spirit washes over us in mind-transforming love, forgiveness and acceptance.

Ephesians 4:22–24 says:

You were taught, with regard to your former way of life, to put off your old self, which is being corrupted by its deceitful desires; to be made new in the attitude of your minds; and to put on the new self, created to be like God in true righteousness and holiness.

Paul writes that there is a choice we make in putting on or off the identity of God's righteousness. That choice is made in the "attitude of your minds." The word for "attitude" there is taken from a Greek root word meaning "spirit" of your mind. It can mean God's Spirit, our spirit or a "movement of air," such as "breath of the nostrils or mouth."[4]

The transformation of our minds is the shifting of our beliefs that limit His abundance for us. It begins with the realization of the goodness of our Father. Our doubts about our value, worth and identity are resolved by the breath of God. It's His love that transforms our minds. He breathes on our minds with His love and kisses us to remind and assure us that He welcomes us not as slaves but as cherished children.

At the instant our will turns toward Him, He starts after us to lavish us. When met by a Father we have rejected, at least in parts of our soul, we know who we are by His demonstration of love and faithfulness. The change is in the way we see Him and how we see us as He sees us. He restores the attitude of our minds to agreement with the love of His Sprit.

The change we experience in the renewal of our mind is the transformation of knowing we are sons where we believed we were slaves. Our agreement with His truth about us and the realization of His love which was there all along changes not only our minds but everything about us.

Points to Consider

- Even where we believe in God as God, we can doubt His place as Father applies to us.

- Doubt is an opportunity for choice which affirms faith.

- The transformation we seek is the exchange of the insecurity of orphans for the security of our place as children of God.

- God's love changes our mind as we are safe to agree with His affirmation of us above the accusations of guilt and shame from the accuser.

- Realizing His steadfast love and faithfulness for us personally, transforms our realization of who He is and who we are in Him.

Chapter 7

THE INNER LAYER OF EMOTION

At one time I was ministering weekly in a youth prison. When I would meet new inmates, I would introduce myself and ask their name; just try to begin engaging them in some semblance of a conversation. These wounded young men consistently maintained a defensive and disinterested posture as they barely answered my question. Next, I would ask where they were from and their posture and response were almost identical to what they were to the first question. It was the third question that got them.

"Where is your father?" was the question that changed everything. With that question, the young man's head would come up, and his eyes would connect with mine for the first time. Inside his eyes, I could see the question he would never ask: "How did you know?"

From there, he would tell me his father story, which was always terrible, and I would usually respond with a healthy, affirming touch by placing my hand on his shoulder. I would look at him and tell the young man something like, "I'm sorry your father failed you. That's not how it's supposed to be."

Every time—and I mean every time—the young man would respond with "It's okay" or "It doesn't matter" or something very similar. Every single time. Without fail, these young men would shrug off their terrible father story, believing their present incarceration and that catastrophic relationship failure had nothing to do with each other. In truth, their current confinement in prison and the father's failure were directly related.

These were teenage boys, but when I was practicing criminal law and would have similar interactions with adults facing criminal charges, the response was the same. I mean exactly the same. The adult defendants were simply the teenagers fast-forwarded a decade or two. Nothing had changed in them emotionally, and the void of the father was still ruling their negative choices.

Just as their younger counterparts, these men would contend their father's failure didn't factor into their current situation—at first. With some prompting, most would usually admit the painful truth. They felt it. There was an undeniable connection between that point of life-altering pain and their current incarceration.

Even from reasonably healthy and well-intentioned fathers, there is typically some level of unintended neglect or hurt. There is almost always some careless phrase or angry declaration even mature adults carry for decades. The pain gets stuffed down and put away because we love our fathers and usually don't want to blame them.

Excusing, ignoring or justifying the event or the person behind an event doesn't negate the emotion; it just stores it deep within us. That emotion or the culmination of many emotions is coming out sooner or later as gluttony, anger, lust, addiction, codependence or whatever other unhealthy response is our particular unhealthy response of choice.

Comfort from the Comforter Because of Discomfort

Nobody was created an addict; the addiction points back to a legitimate need being filled in an illegitimate manner. Nobody was created an anxious, gluttonous or performance-driven workaholic, but those socially acceptable suburban behaviors are just as much deterrence to our freedom as the methamphetamine user's addiction.

When we go through a painful event, we have an emotional mark of that experience. To ignore the reality of feelings associated with such events takes a toll on our emotional health over time. After years of jamming emotions down without taking the time to inventory and process them, minor events can result in major responses. These disproportionate emotional responses are the product of years of unrealized, unacknowledged feelings.

Jesus promises the coming of Holy Spirit as "the Comforter" because God knows His children urgently need comfort. The recognition of discomfort and the promise of Holy Spirit as Comforter make it clear that emotions and our emotional management are a genuine part of our original design. If we choose to pervert the methods we use for comfort we do so at the expense of what the Comforter wants to do in that moment with us and for us.

We don't have to travel too many back roads through life to realize shortcuts usually aren't. Shortcuts to emotional comfort never lead to our intended destination of the Father's estate. Instead, they divert us from Freedom Road, leading to places of compromise as we accept lives of scarcity and servitude over our rightful inheritance as children of God.

Shortcuts to emotional comfort run the gamut from diversions as blatantly illegitimate as drug use or pornography to the more subtle detours of workaholism or even religion. Any means we use to cover up or sidetrack our attention away from our discomfort and what the Comforter wants to do through it lead us farther from home. Traveling these shortcuts is the way of the prodigal.

The Source of Our Primal Emotion

Through the temptations of Jesus (which we will examine in-depth in the next chapter), He demonstrates His complete confidence in and contentment with His position as a son. Nothing could entice Him to doubt or forfeit that position.

Unfortunately for you and me, Genesis 3:10 (see Chapter 2) delivers the bad news of our inheritance that Adam bought us a default position not of security and contentment but of insecurity and dissatisfaction. His attained knowledge of good and evil set the prodigal on its rebellious way outside the Father's estate, and Adam became his own god. You and I were born into that same place of small-letter deity.

Since we really aren't equipped to be gods, the net result is insecurity from the self-awareness of our brutally apparent incompetence. We obviously need God, but our default nature of self-reliance leaves a void we perpetually strive to fill. In the dark middle of that void, our insecurities provide fertile ground for fear to grow unchecked.

Without redemption, fear rules as our primary emotion. Regardless of our apparent confidence, we all know we're limited, and therefore compensate in various ways. Scrambling to earn more, to protect ourselves from every conceivable threat or to promote ourselves above our current place sucks us dry of the energy intended to worship and serve our King.

That primal emotion of fear shapes all our thoughts and influences all our choices. From the inside out, we feed our faulty beliefs inherited from the fallen state of Adam. Our insecurities drive our need for affirmation, and we overcompensate in every area of our lives, even our faith.

We find ourselves doing things "for" God instead of "with" God. We seek His approval and promotion through performance from a position of insecurity rather than enjoying the peace and joy of the truth that we're afforded right-standing with Him simply because of Jesus. Fear traps the prodigals in our soul, slopping pigs in a foreign land even as the Father calls us to start home.

Eternally His

Fear and insecurity inevitably result in pride. Pride is self-focus that shows up in more ways than simply bragging or arrogance. While self-promotion can definitely be a result of insecurity, so can self-degradation. Any inward focus at the expense of God's truth leaves us zeroed in on either our strengths or our flaws but certainly distracts us from His truth of our identity.

That's worse than it sounds since James 4:6 tells us, "God opposes the proud but shows favor to the humble." God actively stands against pride; He aggressively fights it. That means if we operate from fear and insecurity, resulting in pride as either arrogance or self-degradation, we will not enjoy God's favor. In fact, we will have to deal with His might. It's the only sin in Scripture with that promise—or rather that warning.

The only force that overcomes the fear in our soul is love. The opposite of fear is love, not courage. Courage requires fear; love overwhelms it. Perfect love casts out fear, and the only love that is perfect is the Father's love (1 John 4:18). His love, demonstrated through the life, death and resurrection of Christ, permeates the depths of our soul to convince us of what we can otherwise never believe: That we are indeed His children.

Born orphans, we are adopted by the Father when we are born again. To understand our place in the Father's house, we need to know what it means to be adopted. In Jewish law, a natural born child could be disowned and cut off from their father's inheritance. Not so with adopted children. Once adopted, they were a child and heir forever. There was no going back on the father's decision to adopt because it was an act of his will to freely choose the adopted child. He could not change his mind—ever.

In the same way, the Father chooses us, and the orphan soul with which we were born becomes part of His family forever. The fear and insecurity of the orphan are replaced with the irrevocable love and security of the adopted child, as Paul wrote, "For those who are led by the Spirit of God are the children of God. The Spirit you received does not make you slaves so that you live in fear again; rather, the Spirit you received brought about your adoption to sonship. And by him we cry, 'Abba, Father.' The Spirit himself testifies with our spirit that we are God's children" (Romans 8:14–16).

Love is the Catalyst

The Father's love flowing through the innermost layer of our soul is persuasive in ways our minds won't rationally conclude, but can agree with. His love wins the day in the battle of the soul where fear otherwise rules unbridled. And while it's necessary for us to understand with our minds and act through our will, it's ultimately His love that will convince us, not our understanding.

As we turn from our sin and head home, the Father doesn't wait for us to prove anything. He runs to us as soon as He sees us. From the estate of His Spirit within our spirit His love rushes over our soul and transforms our fears. He meets us in our fears and fills us with His love that casts out all fear. The result is the security that comes from knowing the love of the Father, and the innermost ring of our soul submits to His overwhelming presence. With submission, there is permission and the love of the Father becomes the catalyst for the transformation that is happening within us.

Points to Consider

- Whether we acknowledge them or not, we have emotional responses to life's experiences.

- An inventory of our emotions affords us the chance to align them with God's love.

- God is, by His nature, a Comforter.

- When we seek comfort in other places, we leave God out of what He desires for us.

- As soon as we repent and head home, the Father runs to us. His love overcomes our emotions to dispel the lies that torment our understanding.

- God is our healer. He will heal our emotions as He transforms our thinking to renew our realization of identity.

Chapter 8

ROBES, RINGS AND SANDALS

My first year of law school, I had a contracts professor who was the most intimidating professor we "One-Ls" faced that initiation year. He was a master at what is called the Socratic Method and would work a given subject and a person's learning of it masterfully by asking one question on top of the other.

The questions he chose surgically peeled back your answer to examine the reason and logic that was used to reach the answer you offered. Through his cross-examination, you would doubt things you swore to be true just minutes before. That was the point: Know the "why" of the conclusions to develop your thinking in order to best advocate the position you represent.

This professor would get most frustrated with students who didn't want to delve as deeply as he was leading them. He would rant when it appeared a student was attempting to skip the logical support to get to what they concluded was the rule of law. The rant was typically something like, "You first-year law students are all the same, 'The rule; just give me the rule.' It's all you think about!"

He was right, but not just about novice law students. We all want rules to follow. We want to know where the boundaries are so we can stay between the lines. If we know what to do, we'll do it and then we will be accepted or approved of based on our following the rules. The rules and boundaries make it easier to gauge our performance.

Performance is effort under the law. A life of grace liberates us to purpose. Performance is reverse engineering our behavior to look like the thing we want to be. Grace allows us to simply be it. The Father desires children walking in purpose to establish His Kingdom, not servants performing for the sake of appearance or approval. There's no freedom in pretending or striving to "be"; freedom is realized in the flow of authentic life that happens when we agree with our identity and operate from it.

Who Are You?

In Matthew 3, Jesus is baptized and comes up from the water hearing His Father say, "This is my beloved Son, with whom I am well pleased." Before He ever begins His ministry or accomplishes His destiny, the Father affirms Him as a son. He doesn't have to earn it by doing things "for" God or first be "used by" God. Jesus is affirmed as a son based on His lineage, not His performance. Jesus is affirmed based on His identity, just as the Father is willing to affirm us based simply on who we are. He approves us and affirms us based on who we are as we are who He designed us to be.

From His baptism and that affirmation as God's Son, Jesus is led into the wilderness for a time of testing. Not testing in the sense of pass/fail or good/bad, but testing in the sense of proving or refining, similar to the process of refining metal of its impurities. Jesus didn't have impurities, but we do. He was submitting to a process He didn't need to make a way for the process we must go through.

In Matthew 4, after 40 days of fasting, at a time when He was weak and hungry, there are three temptations presented to Jesus:

- "If you are the Son of God, tell these stones to become bread" (v. 3).

- "'If you are the Son of God,' he said, 'throw yourself down. For it is written: 'He will command his angels concerning you, and they will lift you up in their hands, so that you will not strike your foot against a stone'" (v. 6).

- "Again, the devil took him to a very high mountain and showed him all the kingdoms of the world and their splendor. 'All this I will give you,' he said, 'if you will bow down and worship me'" (vs. 8–9).

Notice the questions in the first two temptations. At first we think the temptation was to turn stones into bread to satisfy His physical hunger or jump off a building and call down angels to prove His divinity. Those were certainly actions tempted in the wake of the actual question, but the question was more fundamental and pivotal to Jesus' ministry: "If you are the Son of God." The question was, "Do you know who you are?" The same question continually tempts us. The answer we give is just as pivotal to our destiny.

If we don't know who we are, we can't overcome the temptations. Unless we're confident of our identity as children of God, reminded by His Spirit's testimony with our spirit, we will be stuck forever living from Adam's legacy position of small "g" god of our life, never attaining or enjoying the abundant blessings of sonship. It's the Father's gentle reminders at our core that equip us to work out His salvation within us.

A Case of Imparted Identity

God is Spirit so He speaks directly to our spirits, deep calling to deep. When we hear His voice, we know our true identity at the core of our being, but if we're unwilling or unable to hear the Spirit's deep call, we become confused and deceived by the lies of an enemy that accuses us from our own flaws. Unless we're connected to the Source of identity that overcame the sin of our humanity, we'll look at our flawed soul and think we are what we do. We'll sit sullenly forever in a circle with others and let the world label us "convicts."

Identity is eternal and not based on our performance, or we're all sunk. We get to be children of God and co-heirs with Christ because of Christ. We get to be something we could never otherwise be simply because He gives it to us. From the identity He has imparted, we can walk in the truth of how He originally designed us.

From the question of identity, the temptations call to the limitations of our souls. The temptations center around three basic drivers of human nature:

- Provide for yourself: Turn the rock into bread to feed yourself.
- Protect yourself: Jump off the building and summon angels to rescue you.
- Promote yourself: Bow down and gain authority.

Without the assurance that the Father will provide for us, protect us and promote us, we will work from the anxiety of doing for ourselves. Our identity will increasingly become wrapped around our measures of success in those three areas. As such, our identities will increasingly become about us and validated by tangible signs of our self-protection, self-provision and self-promotion. We will be our own little gods, no matter what we do on Sunday mornings.

The first two temptations are preceded with "If you are the Son of God." The third temptation regarding promotion to receive authority and glory doesn't question identity. It isn't a question of being a son of God; it's a question of being satisfied with that place. This third temptation is the same one that caused Lucifer to fall and become Satan. It's the same temptation many of us face to replace Kingdom Purpose with the American Dream.

Each temptation brings results that are satisfying for a season as we generally are able to provide for ourselves to some measure and protect ourselves to some degree. We also can achieve accomplishments to a point which makes us feel capable beyond the need for God. The weight of the place that only He is intended to fill, however, eventually crushes even the seemingly strongest of us. The idol of "me" is always destined for destruction.

The Benefits of Identity

The Spirit of God at our core works His way out through our soul, from the inner ring of emotion, through our mind, into our will, finally overtaking our flesh. It's an inside-out realization of our identity, not an outside-in management of our behaviors. We typically (and religiously) try to change our behaviors (flesh) to reflect what we think we ought to be so others believe we are "good." We aren't good; Jesus is. We can never be "good enough" to solve the problems of our behaviors in and of our own disciplines. Only in letting go the prideful need to perform and letting Jesus be our good, at our very core where He resides, can we authentically represent Him.

Attempting to "act like" a Christian according to what we perceive a Christian is inflames the turmoil of the war in which our spirit and the prodigals already are engaged. Our flesh is not naturally going to want to accept the invitation to glory God's Spirit offers. Fellow freedom-quester Paul experienced this battle and recorded his counsel in Galatians 5:17: "For the flesh desires what is contrary to the Spirit, and the Spirit what is contrary to the flesh. They are in conflict with each other, so that you are not to do whatever you want." Trying to will our fleshly desires into "being good" only fuels a conflict from which we will never find rest through our striving.

When the prodigal son of Luke 15 had enough of the consequences of his poor choices, he got up and headed back to his father's house. The same invitation home is extended to the prodigal places in our soul. When we've had enough of doing things our way and eating with the pigs, we can go home. The Father will have compassion and run to meet us. As James 4:8 says, when we come close to Him, He comes close to us.

Most of us perceive our place in the Father's house exactly as the prodigal of Luke 15 when he took his first step onto the road home. We know categorically where we've been and what we've done. More than that, we know how resolutely we've rejected a good and loving God. Crawling back into the servant's quarters to eat the crumbs from the Father's table appears merciful and bountiful in light of our "record." Such a fate is exponentially better than cuddling up with pigs in a pigsty.

Our mindset as we head to the House is "I am no longer worthy to be called your son; make me like one of your hired servants" (Luke 15:19), but the Good Father has no plans for us to be servants. He will have nothing less than restored children. Servants perform. Sons and daughters simply are. Servants strive to provide, protect and promote themselves. Sons and daughters live peaceably and joyfully with their Father and inherit the Kingdom.

The Father has purposes for His children to fulfill in furtherance of His Kingdom. When we return to Him from whatever form of rebellion we've entertained, He equips us to carry out the things that He's designed for us. He offers us:

- **The best robe**—not just any robe but the best robe, an indicator of identity. We are not just put back in place, but put in the best place. He establishes our place as children with rights to an inheritance. He gives us what is His to appropriate as ours.

- **A ring on our finger**—as a symbol of authority. He confers to us the place of royalty and the authority that goes with it. We are commissioned as ambassadors of Heaven on earth and walk in the authority of the Father. Darkness trembles at the legitimate authority of Jesus we have been given to carry out His purposes.

- **Sandals on our feet**—because only slaves go without shoes and we are not slaves. We are not slaves to the law, serving a taskmaster God. We are not slaves to sin as we submit the prodigals in our soul to the Spirit of adoption. We are sons with a place in the house through the sacrifice of Jesus.

We must know who we are from our core to avoid the traps of insecurity that come from a false sense of identity. This is important because it's the center circle of our being. Realizing who we are and what we get as a result provides us with the security needed to walk in love. Insecurity fosters fear and promotes pride to overcompensate but love fuels humility. Humility is the posture from which we recognize then multiply the Father's love. It's the only posture through which His glory can be revealed through us.

Points to Consider

- We don't have to strive to perform but instead can rest in the provision of a son.

- We are not disqualified from our place as sons in the house of God based on our behaviors, not even our rebellion.

- Consequences are our friend; the prodigal needs to know the results of rebellion to value the benefits of submission.

- The kindness of God in His provision and abundance are attractive compared to the absence of His goodness in our circumstances where we have rejected Him.

- When we come home to Him in areas of our lives where we were distant, we come home in our identity as His children, not as well-behaved slaves.

- Our inheritance is forever available; it does not diminish with our mistakes.

Chapter 9

FREEING THE PRODIGAL

Why would we leave the comfort and security of the Father's love which dwells within us? Why do we do the things we hate, just as Paul confessed in Romans 7:15? We are born again, adopted children of a Father God who loves us unconditionally and has a home of abundance He freely offers us, yet we roam. Why? The answer is in our prodigal soul.

As we live, life happens. We experience things. Those experiences create emotional responses, some good, some not so good, some blatantly bad. No matter how demonstrative or stoic we are, there are emotions produced from life's experiences. Those feelings may not be acknowledged or expressed, but they are present just the same. Left unacknowledged, they are stuffed down inside us, one piling on top of the other.

These hurts and our responses might have occurred before our salvation, but the strongholds they create reside in our soul even after the Father resides in our spirit. They could also come after salvation when the pain of our soul supersedes our acknowledgment of His available comfort. In either case, we facilitate a reaction to avoid that pain in the future. The prodigal soul attempts to comfort past hurts and the potential for future pain by running to alternatives instead of turning home.

Uncovering the Lie to Uproot the Stronghold

As we saw in a previous chapter, our will is easy to determine because it always shows up in our behaviors. The easiest way to determine whether we're home, hearing the testimony of Holy Spirit with our spirit regarding our identity in a given moment is to look at the choices we're making. If we're making unhealthy, disruptive or destructive choices, choices that contradict the character of our Father, it's safe to say we're not working from an identity rooted in the affirmation of Holy Spirit.

Our will shows itself in our behaviors, and our behaviors reveal our beliefs, particularly about our identity and about God; therefore, if we look at our choice in a given circumstance, we can back up to examine the belief behind the decision we made. We can continue the process to consider whether or not that belief is true or a lie and then where it originated. It looks like this:

If you need encouragement for why you should read the Bible, here it is. You can't know the truth from a lie if you aren't familiar with the truth. Where there is a lie

FREEING THE PRODIGAL | 81

impacting our beliefs, we can redeem it and walk free from the bad choices born from false beliefs based on lies that create strongholds. That's what repentance is: Changing our mind to agree with the truth and walking in our identity as sons.

Connecting the Dots

I once represented a young woman charged with possession of illegal drugs. She was going to serve time in jail and was understandably upset at the unavoidable consequences she faced. Her problems were compounded by the fact she'd been in the same trouble several times previously. One day I decided to question her about her drug use.

"Why do you keep using?" I asked in the hallway of the courthouse.

"I'm addicted" she responded.

I followed up with a simple question, "Why?"

She didn't know why, so I asked her, "Can I ask you just one final question?" With her permission, I asked plainly, "Where is your family?"

"My mom is about to go to prison, and I don't have a dad."

Even as the final "d" of "dad" hung in the air, she completely broke down. She went from upset to hysterical. The hurt of her reality came rushing up and out and all over the place, right there in the courthouse hallway.

Bad choices are driven by wounded souls. I helped this young woman connect the dots between the hurt arising from abandonment by her father and her use of drugs to mask that pain. We worked backward from her choices (drug use) to beliefs (nobody loves me) to at least an initial and primary lie regarding her worth.

In the wound of her father's abandonment, the lie that she was worthless and unlovable took root. It became her truth, her identity. The heartbreaking pain of that "truth" demanded comfort. She found that comfort in drugs and her addiction and the horrible consequences that ensued fed the lie of worthlessness she'd adopted as truth, and the stronghold was perpetually reinforced.

This young woman had to "go there" to realize it was there. Her first thought regarding the "why" of addiction was about her body's acquired need for drugs, not the wounding of her soul and the resulting false beliefs. She couldn't' even want the healing she didn't know was necessary.

Wounds Empower Strongholds

The majority of the time stronghold-producing lies take root in a wound. We tend to form beliefs to self-protect following the experience of hurt or disappointment. To avoid repeating the pain, we believe lies that limit our perception of God, of ourselves or both. In the wake of the pain, we conclude we can do a better job as god in the area we've been injured.

Being unwilling to risk vulnerability, we determine we can control our outcomes better than He did. We choose to self-protect, self-provide and self-promote. We become Adam all over again, choosing to rely on our own resources rather than the Source for our protection, provision and promotion. The results of this lie-born idolatry are increasingly sinful choices and progressively more detrimental consequences, and the spiral of depravity begins.

We continue to act and react from this idolatrous position until the lie is revealed and we exchange it for the real God and His actual truth. If we ask, Holy Spirit will reveal the lie as well as the pain that are the source of our bad choices. Once revealed, the injuries of our soul can be healed. Once healed, the lie has no place to fester.

Detect and Destroy

While changing our mind can be as simple as deciding to adopt a different belief about God, the soul's cry for an even deeper change is the impetus that gets us from here to there. Courage to pursue truth is necessary to dive into the kind of transformation available that produces freedom from strongholds. Connecting the choices of our will by examining our behaviors raises the all-important question of why we did those things in the first place.

There's an old saying that if you want a better outcome, you need a better effort, but there are limitations to our abilities to break free from strongholds that present persistent traps of bondage in our lives. Strongholds are where the grace of Christ shines most brilliantly because without His grace that leads to repentance and His truth that sets us free we are helpless to detect and destroy the false beliefs that form the foundation of these prisons. Prodigal parts of our soul become trapped in strongholds and lose hope of going home. Christ's grace provides the jailbreak they're waiting for.

Lies rooted in wounds can be replaced with the truth. The truth of the Father's love received in the wake of healing from earthly hurts restores the prodigal part of our soul to the love of the estate of the Father's Spirit within. As we receive truth and healing, we begin walking in healthy choices that free us from the stronghold and lead us home.

Benefits of Redemption

God is in the redemption business. Sometimes to get from here to there requires a couple of the "why" questions we looked at previously to allow Holy Spirit to take us beyond the obvious choices to the beliefs, lies and even hurts that drive those choices so we can exchange them for the hope of a Savior and destroy the stronghold holding us captive.

The "why" begs the question of our belief, which is a product of our mind. We either believe the truth or a lie. There is no third category. That belief, the truth or the lie, was what led to the choice of our will. We do nothing "just because." Every action and every word originate somewhere, and the first somewhere is the belief of our mind, whether true or false.

As we've seen, our mind, our will and our emotions don't operate independently of one another. In fact, it's our emotional responses to our experiences that tell our mind what to believe about those experiences. The message our mind receives from our emotions causes us to form beliefs to avoid pain associated with a particular occurrence. To change our mind, we often have to explore the emotions that informed our mind in the first place and to do that we have to go places that aren't necessarily easy or comfortable.

When we go to places of hurt, we're able to determine the internal messaging we've been championing to self-protect, self-provide or self-promote. Once we make that determination, we can replace our emotionally-rooted misinformation about the experience with the truth, changing our belief and ultimately the choices we make; thus, we begin to dismantle the stronghold, eventually destroying it, releasing the prodigal parts of our soul to head home.

The good news of the Gospel of Jesus is "He has sent me to proclaim freedom for the prisoners and recovery of sight for the blind, to set the oppressed free" (Luke 4:18). He wants to set us free from strongholds and give us a vision for our purpose in a Kingdom that is bigger than us. He is inviting us home to the family business of redeeming a fallen world, and we get to play a role in the unfolding of God's glory.

As God's children, we get to step into freedom and lead others toward freedom. You don't have to have it figured out; you just have to make up your mind you're willing to take the first step. Rest assured, you won't be walking alone.

Points to Consider

- We can carry strongholds of behavior for decades without realizing they are self-protection born of hurts and disappointments.

- Where there is a persistent behavior based on a lie, it is typically rooted in a wound.

- Emotional awareness and an active inventory of those emotions manage wounds before there is a chance to harbor lies that produce strongholds.

- Recognizing persistent depravity and changing our minds leads us to the roots that have created strongholds.

- Where there has been a lie in a wound, the act of acknowledging it allows us the chance to exchange it for the truth and healing.

Chapter 10

ACCEPTING THE INVITATION

I had a young adult client whose mother accompanied him to his court appearance. I'd gone to the prosecuting attorney before our court hearing and was offered a deal for this young man. The prosecutor was willing to recommend that he serve two consecutive weekends in jail in exchange for a guilty plea. Accepting this offer would mean he could keep working throughout the week and life would be rather routine except for the two weekends.

I sat down in the conference room with the young man and his mother and told them the prosecutor's offer. To my amazement, my client starting throwing himself around in his chair, dropping his head into his hands and cursing repeatedly. He cussed and fussed and whined that "I only get to see my girlfriend on the weekends."

I just sat there and watched as he carried on. At one point during the display, his mother attempted to interject, but I raised my hand in a "Stop" gesture and quietly said, "No, we'll wait on him." He finally settled down, lifted his head out of his hands and looked at me.

"Are you finished?" I asked him. "Are you done?

Because that's not going to go well for you in the courtroom. You don't have to take the deal if you don't want to. We can go to trial and try to win. We may win, and if we don't you may or may not end up with a worse punishment than two weekends in jail. It's really your call, but here's the deal: You got yourself into this mess; if you don't own this, you'll repeat the same mistakes."

To his credit, he responded well to the challenge. He ultimately accepted the deal, but more important, he owned the behavior. The consequences of his choices carried him to a place where he was able to choose a different way. He was able to change his mind. He was able to repent and move forward.

Jesus Defeated Our Defeat

Many of us grew up believing repentance is associated with guilt and could be used against us to condemn our behavior as we "need" to repent typically to avoid the wrath of an angry God. Repentance, however, isn't about guilt and condemnation; it is about grace and invitation.

"It is finished," declared Jesus. He did it. He defeated the defeat in our lives, and we don't have to add to His sacrifice with our wailing. We only have to agree with Him and dine at the table He's prepared. Our gaffes and garbage don't disqualify us. His blood isn't that fragile.

John the Baptist challenged others to change their minds. He was the last prophet tending the intersection of law and grace. He called people to repent and prepare to recognize their coming Savior. His ministry was straightforward: "In those days John the Baptist came, preaching in the wilderness of Judea and saying, 'Repent, for the kingdom of heaven has come near'" (John 3:1–2). John was calling others to stop breaking the law in order to enter the coming Kingdom.

Jesus used the same words to complete the transition: "From that time on Jesus began to preach, 'Repent, for the kingdom of heaven has come near'" (Matthew 4:17). Jesus took the handoff at the intersection and moved us from the law to grace. The law went from an external effort to an internal identity. The exact words declared by John as "Stop," as in "Stop breaking the law," were used by Jesus to say, "You're invited." Jesus wasn't just announcing the Kingdom; He was inviting us in.

There is a huge difference between the prohibition of John and the invitation of Jesus. Repentance in the New Covenant of Jesus is an invitation into the Kingdom. God invites us on mission with Him, and in that eternal purpose, the perverse behaviors we might choose otherwise become distasteful. We turn toward home and leave our prodigal ways behind. We don't grit our teeth and try harder to change our behaviors. We have purpose in the journey that reduces the temptations of the prodigal to an afterthought.

Jesus calls us into freedom, purpose and destiny. We aren't called to act right; we're invited to live fully. We don't have to stop; we get to run. We are wired for speed.

Our Ticket Out

The decision to turn and change your mind can't be made in secret, solitude and silence. The choices showing up as a result of the lies and strongholds in your life are tangible, and the turning has to be tangible, as well. Out loud and with someone else, confession is evidence of real repentance. When you can own it, admit it, confess it and repent of it, then it can be exchanged for God's glory.

Those things deep within from which we've longed to be free, that seemed so intimidating and permanent in our lives run like cowards when we speak their names and bring them into the light. We're left standing in victory, amazed at the peace and realizing the heaviness of the chains in contrast to the weightlessness of our new mantle of freedom.

That act of confession and the ensuing realization of our emancipation is what we must remember as the enemy of our soul tries to retake lost ground some time after that battle. He doesn't want us to find our way out of his deceit-driven strongholds in our lives, but through Jesus we have an irrevocable ticket out. Our ticket out is to enter in. Entering in, the sins from which we seek freedom no longer bind us because they can never enter into the Kingdom of Jesus' invitation.

Beyond the Fear

When my son started playing baseball, he did so with no small amount of trepidation. He was seeking his confidence through a very real fear of getting hit by the ball. Throwing and catching didn't scare him, but the coach pitching the ball at him left him much more concerned about getting hit than about hitting.

After practice one night, he told me he was afraid. I initially said to him what every father since Abner Doubleday told their sons, "It won't hurt as bad as you think." That didn't work for me any better than for countless dads since Doubleday. Later that evening, however, things changed.

I was sitting in the living room when my son walked in, and I spontaneously said, "You are very courageous. I know you're facing some fear about getting hit and you're hanging in there. I know it's not comfortable and your courage is taking you through it. I'm proud of you."

He lit up like an LED spotlight. Something happened inside him that showed on his countenance and in his posture. He crossed the living room and gave me a hug. The next night at his first game, he hit well and stood in the batting box without flinching; same for the next game after that. He'd made it beyond the fear.

We're all afraid. Without fear, there's no need for courage. Fear is inevitable. Courage is born from confrontation with the inevitable.

Fear versus Freedom

If there's one thing that's been consistent through my years of working with others in freedom ministry, it's the presence of fear. Frankly, this seems to be particularly true for men. Fear tends to hold people back from stepping into freedom. The inherent challenge is that inasmuch as freedom gives relief from fear, fear must be overcome to realize freedom.

The story told in Luke 8:27–37 of the demoniac of Gerasenes[5] is a revealing illustration of the power of fear versus the promise of freedom. The demon-possessed man Jesus delivered wasn't struggling with one demon. He didn't have just one area of darkness or one addiction from which he needed freeing. A legion is between 3,000 and 6,000. It's safe to say he was the most extreme case of bondage that existed in his community.

This man, who was out of his mind tormented, is set free and everybody knows it. It's a big deal and the whole town goes to the cemetery to see what's happened. The people in the community know how horrific this man's life was, and then they see the power of Jesus. They could easily evaluate the extreme nature of the man's liberation because the man, previously naked and chained up in the cemetery, was now fully clothed, in his right mind and calmly sitting at the feet of Jesus.

It stands to reason the demoniac had been in worse shape than everybody else in town, so whatever "demons" they were personally dealing with should be easy for Jesus by comparison. They had torments of their own, although not nearly as extreme or socially unacceptable as the naked guy in the graveyard. They had problems as everybody has problems and here is Jesus, who apparently can fix their problems.

This should be inviting. They should be lining up to learn more about this Jesus guy. After all, He obviously can make things better. The undeniable testimony of the demoniac is compelling evidence. Their reaction, however, is counter-intuitive. Fear overcomes them, and they ask Jesus to leave. They assess the possibilities, know their needs and send Jesus away.

They choose bondage over freedom. They decide they're better off with the predictability of the pain they've grown accustomed to than the unpredictability of what life might look like on the other side of Jesus. In doing so, they're able to avoid any substantive encounter with Him and literally ask Him to leave.

Weird people, huh? Not really. We are those people. We will embrace our fears and faults and put them aside in a place we don't want Jesus or anybody else to look. We'll use them as substitute identities, and the longer we go with these false labels and the accompanying comforting habits, the more adamant we become about holding onto them.

Heading Home

Accepting Jesus' invitation is exhilarating but also can be formidable. James 4:8 tells us drawing near God instigates the transformation required for us to run, but getting close to the "consuming fire" of God (Hebrews 12:29) can be a fearful proposition. It's fear of the unknown in anticipation that something is going to change in His presence and it's not Him. We'd rather leave God in the fireplace, admiring His sight, sound and smell rather than get close enough to let Him burn off our temporal leg shackles.

Until we trust Him enough to draw so close we feel His soul-searing, bondage-breaking heat, we're stuck admiring Him from a safe, religious distance while the transformation available to children of God eludes us in our perceived safety and comfort. Knowing how God looks, sounds and smells is not co-laboring with Him. It's a Sunday morning observation of what is intended to be ever-increasing intimacy.

When we step toward the home intended for us in any particular area of our lives, our Father isn't looking for the finished product of perfection to prove our worth to determine His response. Our turning away from the lusts and lies that led us to the pig slop draws Him to us. He runs to us then accompanies us as we walk out our choice of repentance.

The Father rushes from our spirit, past our emotions and thoughts, which are transformed by His love even as they consider the journey. His love overflows from our emotions, flooding our minds and finally completely overwhelming our will as the prodigal accepts Jesus' invitation. All condemnation is obliterated because our Father has kissed us, breathed His transformative Spirit upon us and now walks us down Freedom Road toward home.

Points to Consider

- Love doesn't demand; it invites.

- Repentance is accepting an invitation to run, not just

complying with an order to stop.

- Transparency and the courage to admit our faults to another are the first step into freedom.

- By our nature, we're more comfortable with our known "demons" than we are with the unknown we encounter when we embrace freedom.

- God's love displaces fear as we draw near Him.

Chapter 11

WALKING FREEDOM ROAD

The way home is within. We have a Father watching for a return to Him in every aspect of our soul. Once we realize our soul harbors inconsistencies with our inheritance as His children, we can choose to leave those places of compromise. Our place in the Father's house is everlastingly secure. He will run to us and remind us of our identity where we have believed a lie. He loves us extravagantly, and we realize that lavish love when we start home from our prodigal distortions. Our return is a soul-altering realization of the freedom that is ours by second birth.

The trip home won't be down a perpetually smooth road. There may be some potholes along the way, and rest assured where there's a road to freedom there are ditches on either side. We all have the ability to keep life between the lines, but we've all found ourselves in the ditch at one point or another, too.

Freedom Road's ditches have two distinct indicators, depending on which side you find yourself stuck. Regardless of which one it may be, the solution for getting back on the road begins with recognizing the ditch for what it is. We see these two ditches illustrated in the story of the Good Samaritan Jesus tells in Luke 10:30–35.

> *In reply, Jesus said: "A man was going down from Jerusalem to Jericho, when he was attacked by robbers. They stripped him of his clothes, beat him and went away, leaving him half dead.*
>
> *A priest happened to be going down the same road, and when he saw the man, he passed by on the other side. So too, a Levite, when he came to the place and saw him, passed by on the other side.*
>
> *But a Samaritan, as he traveled, came where the man was; and when he saw him, he took pity on him. He went to him and bandaged his wounds, pouring on oil and wine. Then he put the man on his own donkey, brought him to an inn and took care of him.*
>
> *The next day he took out two denarii and gave them to the innkeeper. 'Look after him,' he said, 'and when I return, I will reimburse you for any extra expense you may have.'"*

Diversions from Freedom Road typically land us in one of the following ditches:

- **The Ditch of Isolation**: This is a deadly ditch as it is fraught with whispers of hopelessness. Fellowship with other travelers is imperative because it keeps our eyes forward and focused on the reason for our journey. Losing sight of our purpose leads to losing sight of our worth. When we lose sight of our worth, we lose sight of the One that considers us valuable. Left without vision, we'll perish.

- **The Ditch of Religion**: When we slip into performance for God, we gradually get more and more stuck. He has invited us to walk with Him, not to run ahead of Him and do things to try to impress Him. He's not impressed with our performance but loves the identity He created in us.

An enemy whose intent was to kill, steal and destroy, severely beat the traveler, and then left him on the side of the road in the ditch of isolation. He'd set out on his journey without any authentic, healthy relationships that would allow him to live transparently. He'd surrounded himself with the very people who turned on and attacked him.

We aren't designed to handle attacks alone. Our isolation from like-minded believers to encourage us, sharpen us and watch our blind spots results in landing in the ditch. This lone traveler took a whipping he might have avoided walking in community with others.

After this brutal attack, the law (i.e., performance)

passed by in the figure of a priest and a Levite. As they approached, both crossed over to the ditch of religion. Performance through religion will never rescue from isolation; rather it will dismissively judge the behaviors that leave others isolated.

The ditch of religion is a ditch of insecurity, which manifests as pride and arrogance to hide its deficit. Religion will judge and avoid the problems of the freedom journey, but not stop to get its hands dirty in the details of people's lives.

In contrast, Jesus, in the role of the Samaritan, offered healing by His blood (the wine) and Holy Spirit (oil) to restore the broken traveler from the ditch of isolation. The Good Samaritan picked up the broken traveler, healed him and put him back on Freedom Road toward a place of rest (the inn).

Staying Out of the Ditches

At some point on our journey, we all need a tow out of the ditch. At other points along the road, we have the opportunity to get down in the ditch with a tow rope or just our bare hands and pull a fellow trekker from the miry muck. As we transform to a community of transparent freedom chasers tending the ditches, we'll realize the full potential of the church.

The key to maintaining freedom is recognizing ditch diversions before we skid off the road. If we find ourselves drifting from the center of the lane toward the ditch of isolation, we need to raise our hand immediately and let a fellow freedom-finder help us steer. If we realize we're speeding ahead and trying to out-drive our Navigator, we may be headed toward the ditch of religion, and it's time to back off the accelerator and listen for His next routing instruction.

Any journey can become plagued by moments of fatigue when we become lax in our steering and inadvertently begin to leave the safety of the designated lanes. Diligently staying attuned to the smooth hum of the tires, ready to correct course at the first jolt of the lane markers is how we stay out of ditches.

We absolutely cannot travel Freedom Road alone. We need others. The process of transformation requires open communication with at least a few other people to work things out into the light that we probably prefer to hide in the darkness. When headed toward the ditch, the way to stay the course is by transparent connection with others on a similar journey. We won't suffer the consequences of a crash if we recognize a course correction is needed and raise our hands for help. Calling our darkness out into the light by telling others of the trials, temptations and testing we wrestle with disarms the darkness.

Iron Doesn't Sharpen Itself

You can't work freedom out in a weekend retreat, church service, book or any other programmatic attempt. It takes authentic relationships aligned with eternal purpose to achieve eternal purpose. You and several others trying to live in close relationship often are labeled "accountability partners," but relationships based on accountability are inferior to relationships based on transparency. The difference is more than semantics and is critical to the maturity of the individuals involved.

Key differences between being accountable and being transparent include:

- **Accountability** is an outside-in evaluation often based on performance compared to the "rules." In other words, it can become focused on what sin there has been that indicates a need to "do better."

- **Transparency** is a sharing of the heart. It is exposing things brewing within our soul that are revealed as needing healing, redemption or transformation. That's not performance; it's identity.

- **Accountability** is an external mechanism to achieve modified behavior.

- **Transparency** is motivated by transformation as we seek maturity.

- **Accountability** is confined to a meeting or narrow scope of relationships.

- **Transparency** is a lifestyle that facilitates personal freedom as well as freedom for others as it makes it safe to be real beyond only a few people.

A framework of accountability to start a process of self-awareness is excellent progress toward discipline in areas that have created problems in life. That framework, when nurtured to maturity, takes us from dependence on external measures of performance to heart transformations as we become mature disciples. Without evolution toward the greater realization of identity, we remain tied to the Old Covenant of keeping the law to reflect our ability to adhere to God's precepts as opposed to allowing the law written on our hearts reflect an expression of Him.

Until we get real about the "why," we're reduced to guilt, shame and trying hard in the "what." Jesus announced His ministry as healing broken hearts and setting captives free. He died to liberate us from the bondage that manifests as behaviors, not that we might be more capable of managing those behaviors.

Bounding Overwatch

Transparent relationships are mutually beneficial. Where we walk together with others, we increase in our capacity to walk in our purpose, as do they. We don't know what we don't know, and others with a view of our circumstances are able to see things we are blinded to.

There's a formation and movement technique in armor tactics called the "bounding overwatch." It's a maneuver used when contact with the enemy is certain. It's the slowest method of advance, sacrificing speed for security. In a tank platoon, there are four tanks, and in bounding overwatch, two of the tanks watch over the other two tanks while the watched-over tanks move from one location to another. Then the roles are reversed and the formerly moving tanks set and the originally overwatching tanks advance.

> *And they went to a place called Gethsemane. And he said to his disciples, "Sit here while I pray." And he took with him Peter and James and John, and began to be greatly distressed and troubled. And he said to them, "My soul is very sorrowful, even to death. Remain here and watch" Mark 14: 32–34.*

Jesus was about to die. He was about to die, and He knew it. He went to this place of solitude to seek the Father and He invited these friends to go with Him. Jesus was seeking the comfort and counsel of the Father, and He valued and asked for the consolation and company of these three, as well. Jesus was asking these three friends to pastor Him in a time when He was "greatly distressed and troubled."

We all need overwatch in times when contact with the enemy is certain. Pastors need pastors and everyone who needs a pastor must grow comfortable in their calling *as* a pastor. Peter was a fisherman, not a Seminarian. He had never been to school or worked on a church staff; neither had the others. Still, the Lord put them in place as His pastors for this time of sorrow on the eve of His death.

From Jesus' last hours with His friends we learn

- We all need a pastor sometimes.
- We all are called to pastor at other times.
- Pastor is a verb, not a title.

The only way to prevent the need for overwatch is to avoid contact with the enemy by refusing to advance. For those who choose that option (and many do), enemy contact isn't particularly necessary as they're irrelevant to the battle. The safety of stagnation preserves comfort at the cost of the soul. We're designed for agreement and cooperation in the advance; staying behind destroys that part of us created for passion, contact, overwatch, advance and purpose.

Get Out There

Overwatch is necessary on the battlefield, not at the logistical supply point. The church building is where we meet to be encouraged, equipped and deployed back into battle. Hanging out exclusively at the logistical supply point, we don't need to worry about enemy contact, and eventually we die on the inside. We need to get in the fight because without us in the fight, part of the team is out there without overwatch.

The battlefield is, and was always intended to be, "out there." Out there is the marketplace and the community. We only come "in here" to get ready to go back out there. We're called to walk in the gifts and calling released through and in our freedom. The alignment of our mind, will and emotions with the purposes and plans of God's design for us is mandatory as it equips us for the work of ministry.

I have seen as much or more of the Kingdom of God in jails and courts as I have in any church or ministry setting, and in doing so have come more alive in the purposes of life. In contrast with surroundings void of the Kingdom, evidence of the Kingdom within me becomes clear; likewise, when surrounded by darkness, I more easily identify darkness within my soul. Once I see it, I can turn from it and head home.

With eyes to see, we know the joy and passion that come from agreeing with heaven on earth. That joy and passion give us courage to get in the fight, not solely for our freedom but for the freedom of those we're called to walk beside. We find them in every arena of life. They are waiting for us to step onto the road beside them as they make their way home.

Points to Consider

- Walking out freedom cannot be done alone.

- Walking with others in transparent relationships is the New Covenant.

- The Old Covenant, the law of death, prevented transparency and commanded adherence to unattainable edicts.

- Trying to keep the law or living in isolation steals the joy of purpose and destiny inherent in our design.

- As we walk in freedom, we carry it with us to everyone we are in contact with, inside and outside the church.

FINAL CHARGE

There was a time a few years ago that Holy Spirit moved me to share something with a friend. The prompting was to share about an argument my wife and I had been in several weeks prior. I had said ugly things and acted like a jerk.

Following the argument, I had turned away from that behavior and repaired the relationship with her. I had confessed it to others and was not living in solitude or wearing the mask of apparent perfection. It was over and behind me; so why was God prompting me to share it now?

After some back and forth of hesitation and reservation, I met up with this friend. He had just gotten off of the phone, and I began to share the thing I felt I was to confess to him, embarrassed and a bit put out with God that this was even happening. As I finished, he took a couple of backward steps and sat on a nearby ledge with a look of amazement.

"I was just on the phone with my wife," he said. "That's exactly what just happened between us."

Wow.

I wasn't sharing for my healing or transparency or accountability or growth. This Holy Spirit-coordinated encounter was about him. Actually, it was about us. We talked and prayed, and he called his wife and made things right.

This was iron sharpening iron even when the first iron didn't want to tell the second iron there had been any dullness. It was radical obedience and miraculous redemption. It was real and raw and sweet and hard. It was freedom.

As we work our way through life's trials and the triumphs, what if it's not really about us? Would that change our attitude toward suffering and humble us where we might be tempted to pride? What if we are just a means to an end, and the universe doesn't revolve around us after all?

Judges 3:1–2 says:

> *These are the nations the Lord left to test all those Israelites who had not experienced any of the wars in Canaan (he did this only to teach warfare to the descendants of the Israelites who had not had previous battle experience).*

Nobody likes war. Its bloody and dark realities are without any real winners when experienced from the most intimate perspectives. Even the victors carry a lifetime of emotional baggage and difficult memories. The horror of suffering and death in war are real on a scale only those who've experienced it firsthand understand. I'm sure it exceeds even the best attempt of any movie or book to capture its essence. Participants are changed forever.

According to Judges 3, God chose to allow a generation to experience the struggle of war not for the sake of the war itself or even for what He was doing in the generation going through the experience. The intent was "only" so the generations that followed this battle-tested generation would benefit from the experience.

We go through the battle for freedom to benefit the generations that follow. The way we make for them will either accommodate their destiny or frustrate their passions. We have the opportunity daily to stand in the gap for those that follow.

It doesn't take bullets and bombs to constitute combat and strife. We face contention every day and consider escape more than once. It's not about us, though. The benefit to a warrior is not for the warrior; it's for generations the warrior may never know.

Freedom is the realization, appropriation and multiplication of grace. It's simply receiving what Jesus so freely offers. He invites us into the advancement of His Kingdom and our invitation is because of grace. Grace fuels the journey down Freedom Road to the Father's house. We get from here to there only by grace. Grace provides everything we need, and grace has a name. His name is Jesus.

ENDNOTES

[1] Retrieved at https://www.blueletterbible.org/lang/lexicon/lexicon.cfm?Strongs=H5315&t=KJV, (Oct. 2016).

[2] Retrieved at http://biblehub.com/interlinear/jeremiah/17-9.htm, (Oct. 2016).

[3] "Now faith is the substance of things hoped for, the evidence of things not seen."

[4] Retrieved at http://biblehub.com/greek/4151.htm, (Nov. 2016).

[5] "When Jesus stepped ashore, he was met by a demon-possessed man from the town. For a long time this man had not worn clothes or lived in a house, but had lived in the tombs. When he saw Jesus, he cried out and fell at his feet, shouting at the top of his voice, 'What do you want with me, Jesus, Son of the Most High God? I beg you, don't torture me!' For Jesus had commanded the impure spirit to come out of the man. Many times it had seized him, and though he was chained hand and foot and kept under guard, he had broken his chains and had been driven by the demon into solitary places. "Jesus asked him, 'What is your name?' "'Legion,' he replied, because many demons had gone into him. And they begged Jesus repeatedly not to order them to go into the Abyss.

"A large herd of pigs was feeding there on the hillside. The demons begged Jesus to let them go into the pigs, and he gave them permission. When the demons came out of the man, they went into the pigs, and the herd rushed down the steep bank into the lake and was drowned.

"When those tending the pigs saw what had happened, they ran off and reported this in the town and countryside, and the people went out to see what had happened. When they came to Jesus, they found the man from whom the demons had gone out, sitting at Jesus' feet, dressed and in his right mind; and they were afraid. Those who had seen it told the people how the demon-possessed man had been cured. Then all the people of the region of the Gerasenes asked Jesus to leave them, because they were overcome with fear. So he got into the boat and left."